This edition first published in MMXX by
Book House

Distributed by Black Rabbit Books
P.O. Box 3263
Mankato, Minnesota 56002

Cataloging-in-Publication Data is available
from the Library of Congress

Printed in the United States
At Corporate Graphics,
North Mankato, Minnesota

9 8 7 6 5 4 3 2 1

ISBN: 978-1-912904-24-2

Additional illustrations:
Carolyn Scrace, Andy Patching, and Shutterstock.

Consultant: John Cooper studied Geology at university and began a career in museums, specializing in the study of dinosaur fossils at Leicester Museum, England, and the Carnegie Museum in Pittsburgh, USA, before moving to Brighton, England to become Keeper of Natural Sciences at the Booth Museum of Natural History. He is the founder and chairman of the Brighton & Hove Geological Society and has written many children's books on geological themes. He retired in 2015 but remains the Emeritus Keeper of Natural Science at the Booth Museum.

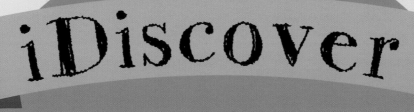

iDiscover

DINOSAURS

and Other Prehistoric Creatures

Written by
Carolyn Scrace

Illustrated by
Liza Lewis

Consultant
John Cooper

BOOK HOUSE
a SALARIYA *imprint*

Contents

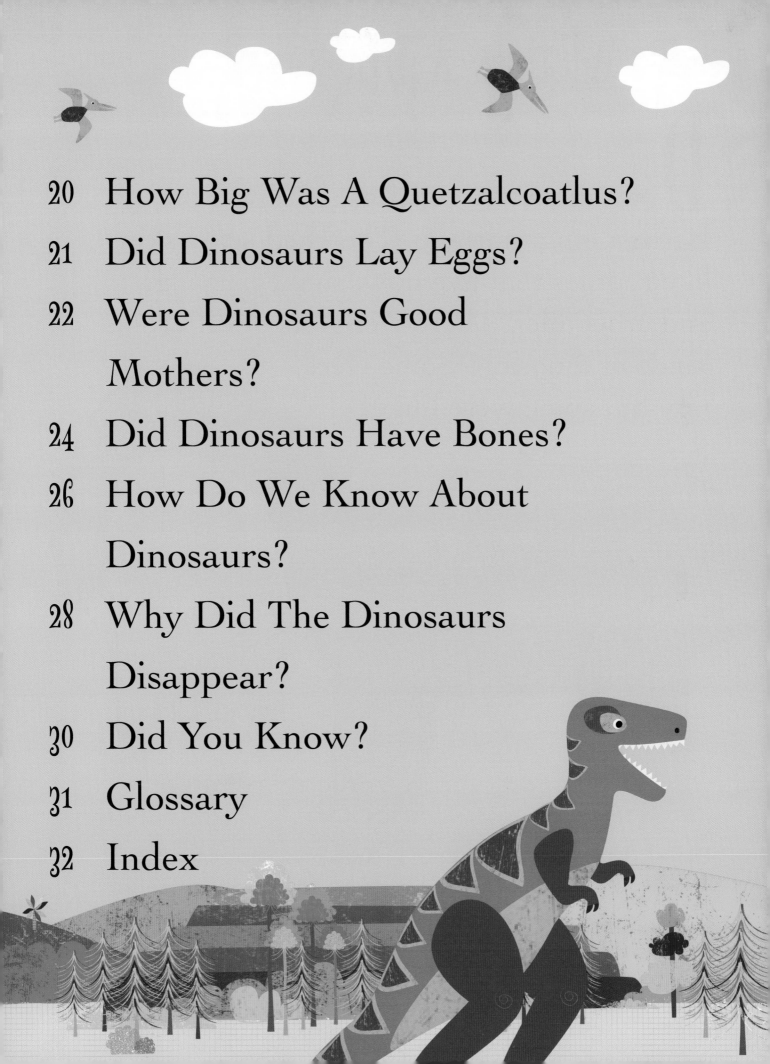

What Is A Dinosaur?

Dinosaurs were **reptiles** that lived on Earth a long time ago. They had scaly skin like reptiles that live now: snakes, lizards, and crocodiles. There were lots of different kinds of dinosaur. Some were tiny but some were huge!

Diplodocus
(DIP-low-DOC-us)

Troodon
(TROH-oh-don)

Diplodocus was a plant-eating dinosaur. It was about 88 feet (27 meters) long and weighed about the same as a large truck.

Troodon, a small dinosaur, was about 7.9 feet (2.4 meters) long and weighed about 99 pounds (45 kilograms).

When Did Dinosaurs Live?

Dinosaurs lived on Earth between 230 million and 65 million years ago. This huge span of time is called the **Mesozoic** Era.

Other Animals That Lived In The Mesozoic Era

Many different animals, including insects, lizards, crocodiles, birds, furry mammals, and fish lived during this time, too—but there were no people then.

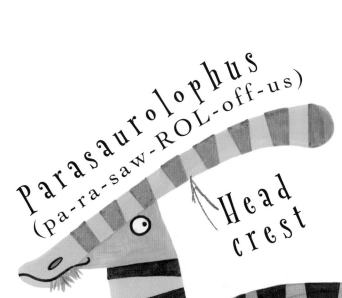

Parasaurolophus
(pa-ra-saw-ROL-off-us)

Head crest

Parasaurolophus was a plant-eating dinosaur. It was about 33 feet (10 meters) long and its head crest was about the size of a man.

What Did Dinosaurs Eat?

Like most creatures living today, dinosaurs were either meat-eaters or plant-eaters. Plant-eating animals are called **herbivores**.

Stegosaurus was a herbivore that lived in North America during the **Jurassic** period.

Stegosaurus was big but it had a brain the size of a walnut.

Stegosaurus
(STEG-oh-SORE-us)

Brachiosaurus
(BRAK-ee-oh-sore-us)

Brachiosaurus was a huge, plant-eating dinosaur. It was about 85 feet (26 meters) long and weighed about 77,161 pounds (35,000 kilograms). It would probably eat up to 880 pounds (400 kilograms) of plants each day.

Swallowing Stones?

Dinosaurs like Brachiosaurus and Stegosaurus may have swallowed large stones called **gastroliths**. These stones helped to grind tough plants into a paste in their stomachs.

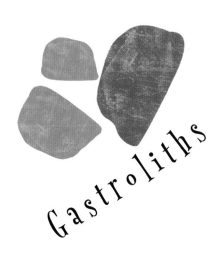

Gastroliths

Grrr! Grrr!

Did Dinosaurs Eat Each Other?

Yes. Huge meat-eating dinosaurs did hunt and eat other dinosaurs. Meat-eating animals are called **carnivores**. Animals that eat plants and meat are called **omnivores**.

Albertosaurus
(al-BERT-oh-saw-russ)

Albertosaurus grew up to 30 feet (9 meters) long and was about the same weight as a car.

Albertosaurus was a carnivore that lived in North America in the late **Cretaceous** period. It had two small hands with only two fingers, a huge head, and a mouthful of sharp teeth. Although big, Albertosaurus could run up to 20 miles per hour (32 kilometers per hour).

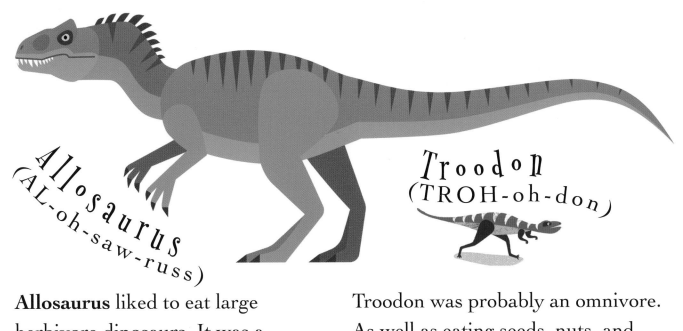

Allosaurus
(AL-oh-saw-russ)

Troodon
(TROH-oh-don)

Allosaurus liked to eat large herbivore dinosaurs. It was a **scavenger**, so it fed on animals that were already dead. Scientists believe it may have fought with Stegosaurus.

Troodon was probably an omnivore. As well as eating seeds, nuts, and fruit, it also ate smaller animals and dinosaurs.

King Tyrant

Tyrannosaurus rex means "king tyrant lizard." It was one of the largest meat-eating dinosaurs that ever lived. It weighed between 19,841–30,864 pounds (9000–14,000 kilograms) and was larger than a bus.

Tyrannosaurus rex
(tie-RAN-oh-sore-us rex)

The skull of a Tyrannosaurus rex measured up to 5 feet (1.5 meters) long. The biggest Tyrannosaurus rex tooth ever found was 12 inches (30 cm) long!

11

What Was The Deadliest Dinosaur?

Spinosaurus was the largest meat-eating dinosaur known to have existed. Unlike other dinosaurs, Spinosaurus must have been **semi-aquatic** (partly water-dwelling).

Spinosaurus's head and teeth were shaped like a crocodile's. Its broad feet and flat claws were ideal for paddling in water.

This deadly dinosaur would have eaten sharks and crocodiles, as well as land animals.

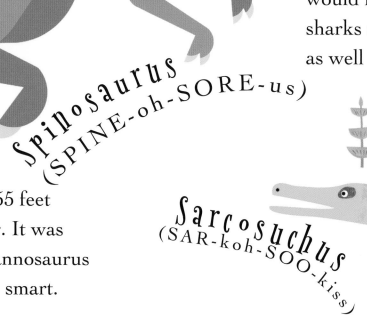

Spinosaurus (SPINE-oh-SORE-us)

Sarcosuchus (SAR-koh-SOO-kiss)

Spinosaurus was 55 feet (16.8 meters) long. It was bigger than a Tyrannosaurus rex but was not as smart.

Were Dinosaurs Bigger Than Elephants?

Yes! Some dinosaurs were even bigger than buses. They were the biggest land-living animals on Earth.

Apatosaurus lived in the Jurassic period and was one of the biggest dinosaurs. It was about 75 feet (23 meters) long and weighed about the same as four big African elephants.

It took an Apatosaurus around 10 years to grow to its full size.

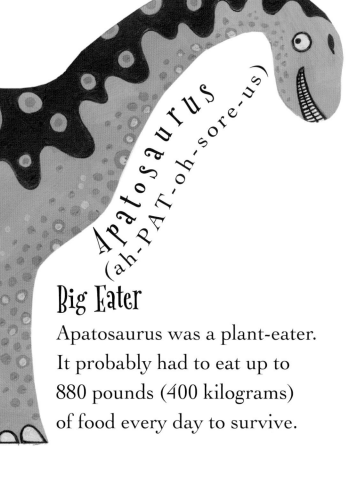

Apatosaurus
(ah-PAT-oh-sore-us)

Big Eater

Apatosaurus was a plant-eater. It probably had to eat up to 880 pounds (400 kilograms) of food every day to survive.

Did Dinosaurs Swim?

Dinosaurs could not swim, but they probably liked to cool off in lakes or rivers. Some reptiles that lived at the same time as dinosaurs, like **plesiosaurs** and **ichthyosaurs**, could only live in water.

Plesiosaurus
(PLEE-see-o-SAWR-uhs)

The **Plesiosaurus** was not really a dinosaur—it was a **Cretaceous** marine reptile with four big flippers.

Diplodocus

Ammonite
(AM-mon-ITE)

Ammonites were **molluscs** that lived in the sea. They scooted along by squirting water from their body to push them forwards.

Placochelys
(PLACK-o-KELL-iss)

Placochelys was a small, turtle-like marine reptile. It had bony plates on its back to protect it. This reptile ate shellfish and had strong jaws and teeth to crush the shells.

Ichthyosaurus
(ICK-thee-o-SAWR-uhs)

Squid

Ichthyosaurus looked like a fish but was a marine reptile. It was about 6 feet (1.8 meters) long. It did not lay eggs, but gave birth to live young.

Squid and fish were a major food source for Plesiosaurus and Ichthyosaurus.

What Animals Lived In Water?

The ancestors of many of today's creatures such as alligators and sharks lived in the seas during the **Jurassic** and **Cretaceous** periods.

Dolichorhynchops
(DO-lick-o-RIN-cops)

Dolichorhynchops was a plesiosaur. Its wing-like flippers made it a fast swimmer.

Styxosaurus
(STICKS-oh-SORE-us)

Styxosaurus was a long-necked plesiosaur. Its neck was over 20 feet (6 meters) long. It didn't chew its prey but swallowed it whole.

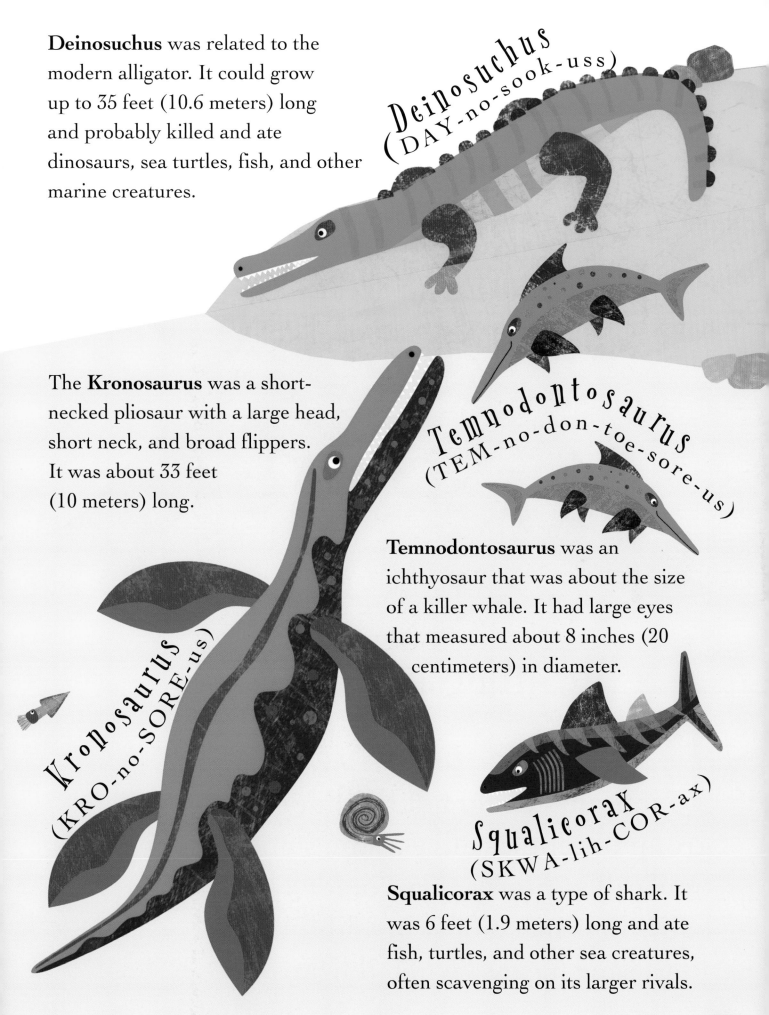

Deinosuchus was related to the modern alligator. It could grow up to 35 feet (10.6 meters) long and probably killed and ate dinosaurs, sea turtles, fish, and other marine creatures.

Deinosuchus
(DAY-no-sook-uss)

The **Kronosaurus** was a short-necked pliosaur with a large head, short neck, and broad flippers. It was about 33 feet (10 meters) long.

Temnodontosaurus
(TEM-no-don-toe-sore-us)

Temnodontosaurus was an ichthyosaur that was about the size of a killer whale. It had large eyes that measured about 8 inches (20 centimeters) in diameter.

Kronosaurus
(KRO-no-SORE-us)

Squalicorax
(SKWA-lih-COR-ax)

Squalicorax was a type of shark. It was 6 feet (1.9 meters) long and ate fish, turtles, and other sea creatures, often scavenging on its larger rivals.

Pteranodon lived near the coast and mainly ate fish and squid. It was as large as a hang glider and had wings measuring over 20 feet (6 meters) from tip to tip.

Pteranodon
(Ter-an-odon)

Did Dinosaurs Fly?

Dinosaurs could not fly, but a group of reptiles alive at the same time called **pterosaurs** could. They had wings made of skin and fur. Pterosaur means "winged lizard."

Pterodactylus
(ter-oh-dak-til-us)

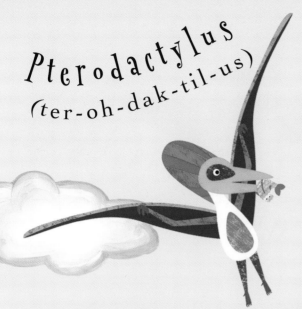

Tapejara
(tah-pay-ZHAR-a)

Tapejara had a head crest that could be up to 3 feet (1 meter) tall.

Pterodactylus means "winged finger." This is because its wing was joined to a long fourth finger on each of its arms. Some species of pterosaurs had a furry coating on their wings, but pterodactylus did not.

Dsungaripterus
(jung-GER-i-TER-us)

Dsungaripterus had a wingspan of about 10 feet (3 meters). It mainly ate shellfish.

Sordes
(SOR-dez)

Sordes only weighed about one pound (450 grams). Its body was covered in fur.

Did Dinosaurs Have Feathers?

Yes. Fossil remains show that many dinosaurs did have feathers.

Quetzalcoatlus
(Kett-zal-coe-at-luss)

Quetzalcoatlus had a very long neck, a sharp, toothless beak, and a long bony crest on its head. With its light body weight and enormous wingspan, it could travel long distances.

How Big Was A Quetzalcoatlus?

Quetzalcoatlus was the largest creature ever to fly. It was the size of a light aircraft and had a wingspan of about 36 feet (11 meters). Its beak alone was even longer than a man!

Did Dinosaurs Lay Eggs?

Many **fossilized** dinosaur eggs have been found. Some dinosaurs, like **Maiasaura**, laid eggs just like birds and reptiles do: they simply scooped out a hole in the ground to make their nest.

The first fossilized dinosaur eggs were found in Mongolia, China, in 1923. They were **Oviraptor** eggs and about the size of a big potato.

Maiasaura
(my-ah-SORE-ah)

Maiasaura

Were Dinosaurs Good Mothers?

Some dinosaurs were good mothers and others were not. Maiasaura, meaning 'good mother lizard', were so named because they seemed to look after their babies well.

Nest Colonies

Large groups of Maiasaura laid their eggs and nurtured their young in nesting colonies. Maiasaura mothers had to watch out for hungry carnivores that might eat their young.

Maiasaura laid batches of around 20 eggs. The eggs were placed carefully in bowl-shaped nests that were about 7 feet (2 meters) wide. Despite the huge size of some dinosaurs, their babies were small—but they grew fast.

Did Dinosaurs Have Bones?

Yes! Dinosaurs did have bones. This is how scientists study dinosaurs. The soft parts of an animal's body rot when it dies. Most dinosaur fossils are the remains of hard body parts like bones and teeth, as well as eggshells and gastroliths.

Fossilized dinosaur

Crocodile

Scientists use their knowledge of existing reptiles, like crocodiles, to work out what kind of muscles and internal organs a dinosaur may have had.

Dinosaur's Tooth

One tooth can be enough to work out what an animal ate. Carnivores have sharp teeth, but herbivores have flat-topped teeth.

Tyrannosaurus rex

Grrr!

Tyrannosaurus rex had over 60 thick, cone-shaped teeth—great for crunching bones!

How Do We Know About Dinosaurs?

Scientists study pieces of fossilized dinosaurs so they can work out what a dinosaur may have looked like. The size of one single bone can be a clue to how big the whole dinosaur may have been.

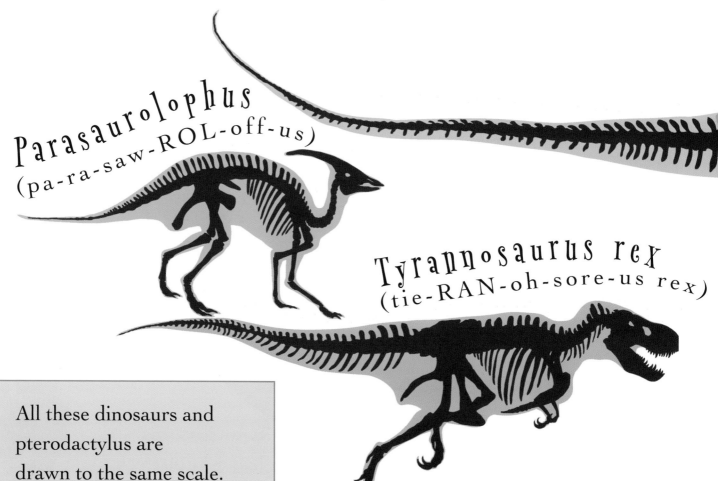

Parasaurolophus
(pa-ra-saw-ROL-off-us)

Tyrannosaurus rex
(tie-RAN-oh-sore-us rex)

All these dinosaurs and pterodactylus are drawn to the same scale.

Paleontologists clear away the rock surrounding a dinosaur fossil to reveal its bones. The bones are carefully removed and transported to a museum. Scientists and artists try to work out what the dinosaur looked like, its size, what it ate, and how it moved.

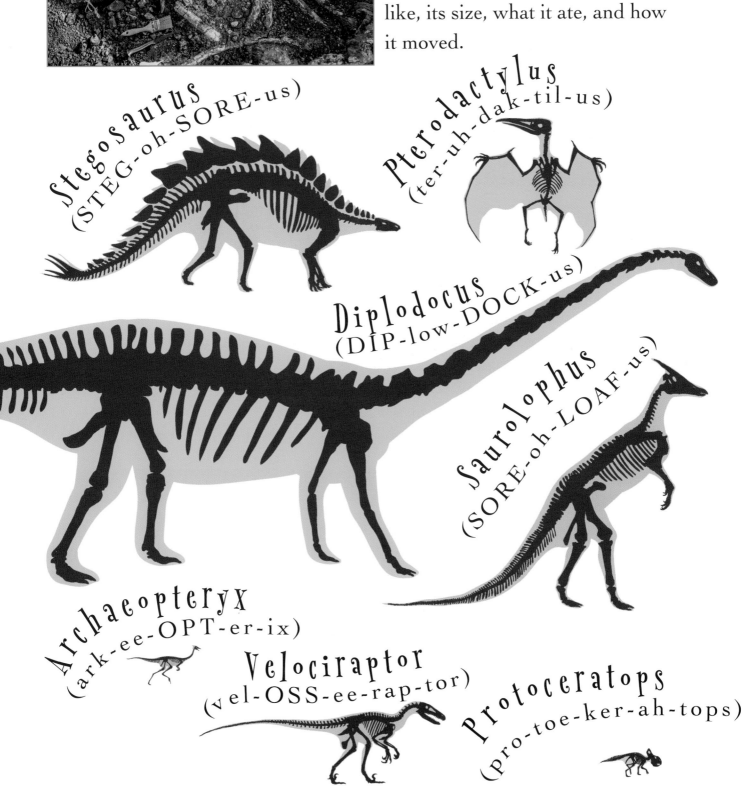

Stegosaurus
(STEG-oh-SORE-us)

Pterodactylus
(ter-uh-dak-til-us)

Diplodocus
(DIP-low-DOCK-us)

Saurolophus
(SORE-oh-LOAF-us)

Archaeopteryx
(ark-ee-OPT-er-ix)

Velociraptor
(vel-OSS-ee-rap-tor)

Protoceratops
(pro-toe-ker-ah-tops)

Why Did The Dinosaurs Disappear?

Dinosaurs suddenly disappeared forever, 65 million years ago. How did this happen? Scientists believe that they were wiped out when a giant **meteor**—a chunk of rock from outer space—smashed into the Earth, causing a huge explosion and a rise in volcanic activity.

Volcanoes

Why Did The Dinosaurs Die?

Gigantic dust clouds and fumes caused by the meteor's impact and volcanic eruptions clogged up the skies. This blocked out all the heat and light from the Sun. The planet was plunged into a cold darkness that probably lasted for months or even years.

Without warmth and light, all plants stopped growing and died. With nothing left to eat, the plant-eaters starved and died. The meat-eaters would have eaten the dead plant-eaters. Once there was nothing left for them to eat—they died, too.

Did You Know?

Dromiceiomimus could run up to 37 mph (60 kph) and looked like an ostrich! It was one of the fastest dinosaurs ever.

The longest name for a dinosaur so far is **Micropachycephalosaurus**.

Seismosaurus, the longest dinosaur, measured over 131 feet (40 meters). That's as long as 5 double-decker buses parked in one line.

So far over 700 different species of dinosaur have been discovered! Scientists believe there are still many more to find.

Many plant-eating dinosaurs had natural weapons to help them fight meat-eaters. **Triceratops** had three horns on its head shield and **Kentrosaurus** had spines along its back and tail.

The smallest dinosaur was **Compsognathus**. When fully grown it was only the size of a chicken.

Many of the biggest plant-eaters ate up to 2,205 pounds (1,000 kilograms) of food a day—that's like eating a pile of vegetation the size of a bus.

The smallest dinosaur egg was only 1.2 inches (3 centimeters) long. The largest eggs were 19 inches (48 centimeters) long.

Therizinosaurus had the longest claws of any dinosaur, they were about 3 feet (1 meter) long.

Dinosaurs lived on every continent, including Antarctica.

The biggest dinosaur skulls were as long as a car.

Triceratops
(tri-SERRA-tops)

Kentrosaurus
(ken-TROH-sore-us)

30

Glossary

Velociraptor
vel-OSS-ee-rap-tor

C

carnivores meat-eaters.

Cretaceous the period from 146 to 65 million years ago. Dinosaurs disappeared at the end of this period.

F

fossilized the remains of a dead animal or plant, naturally preserved in the ground.

G

gastroliths stones swallowed by an animal to help grind up its food.

H

herbivores plant-eaters.

I

ichthyosaurs fish-like, swimming reptiles.

J

Jurassic the period from 208 to 146 million years ago.

M

Mesozoic the period from 248 to 65 million years ago.

meteor a rock from space that hits the atmosphere of the Earth.

M

molluscs soft-bodied animals without skeletons. Some molluscs have shells.

O

omnivores creatures that eat both plants and meat.

oviraptor small, birdlike dinosaur.

P

paleontologist a scientist who studies fossils.

plesiosaurs long-necked, swimming reptiles.

pterosaur a type of flying reptile from the time of the dinosaurs.

R

reptiles animals that lay eggs and use the heat of the Sun to keep their blood warm.

S

scavenger an animal that feeds on dead animals it hasn't killed itself.

semi-aquatic to live partly on land and partly in water.

V

volcanoes mountains with a hole at the top that sometimes spews out rocks, lava, ash, and steam.

Index